My First Colors

BRING ON THE BLUE

MY FIRST COLORS
BRING ON THE BLUE

by Candace Whitman

ABBEVILLE KIDS
A Division of Abbeville Publishing Group
New York London Paris

Bring on the blue!

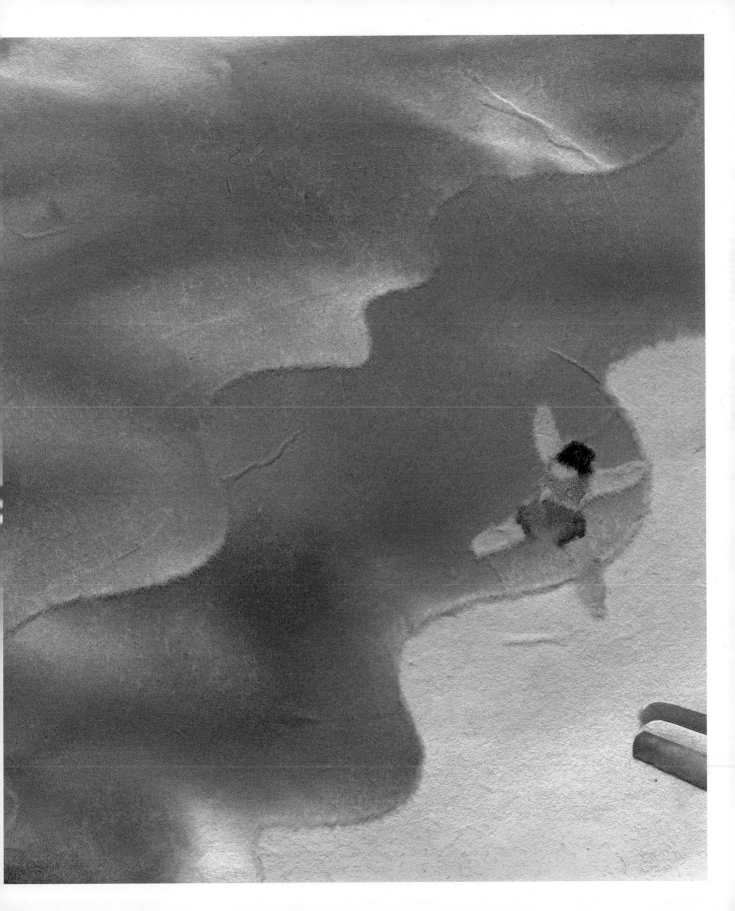

The waves of the sea,

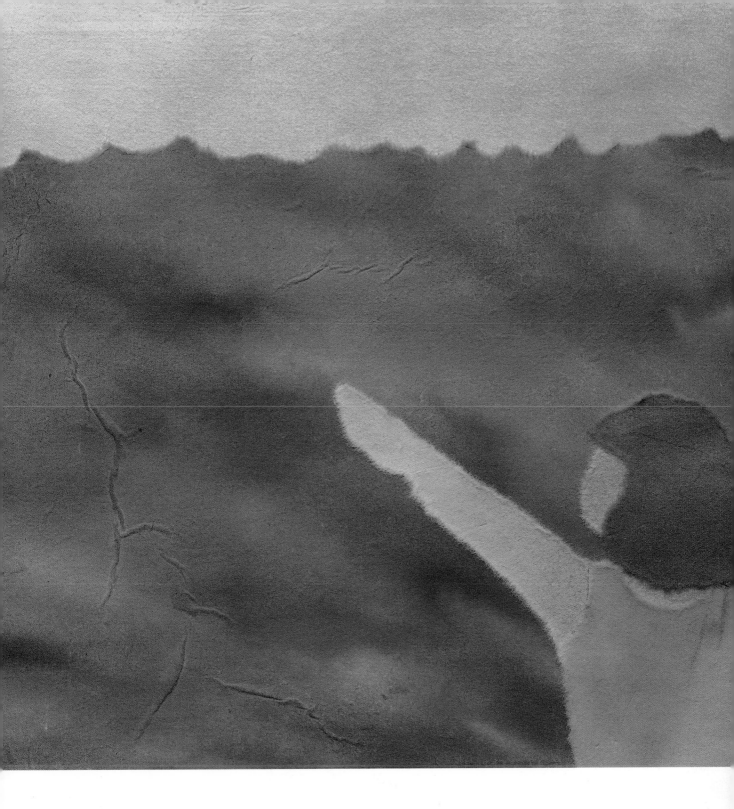

Blue from their very beginning.

And the sea has a twin—
it's the sky above.

Together they bring on the blue!

The sky and the sea
have sisters and brothers.
Do you know where they can be found?

Lining the lane—beautiful bluebells

And in fields of forget-me-nots, too.

Do you know they will always be blue?
It's true.

If you bring on the blue
Shadows come, too.
You've already met some of these.

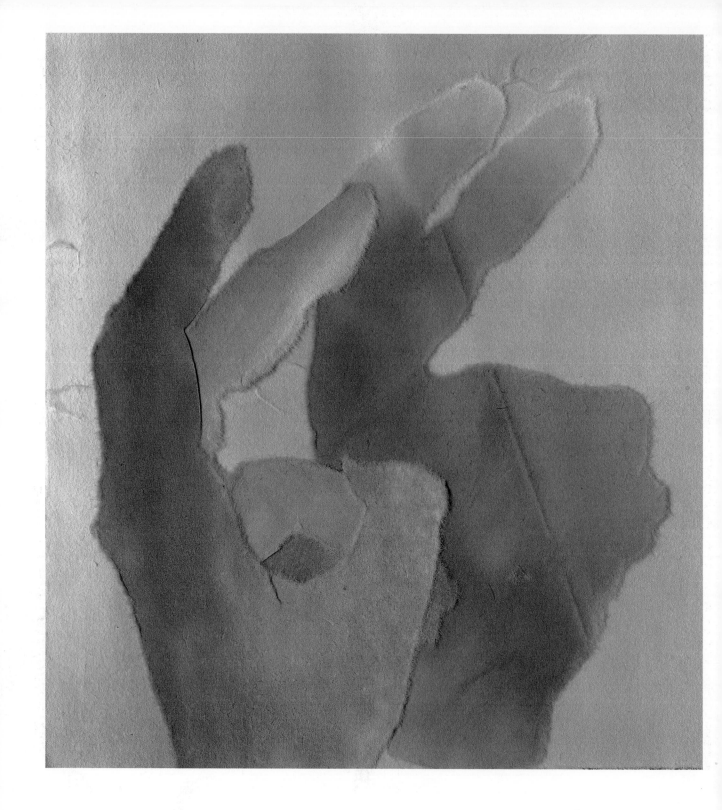

On a wall,

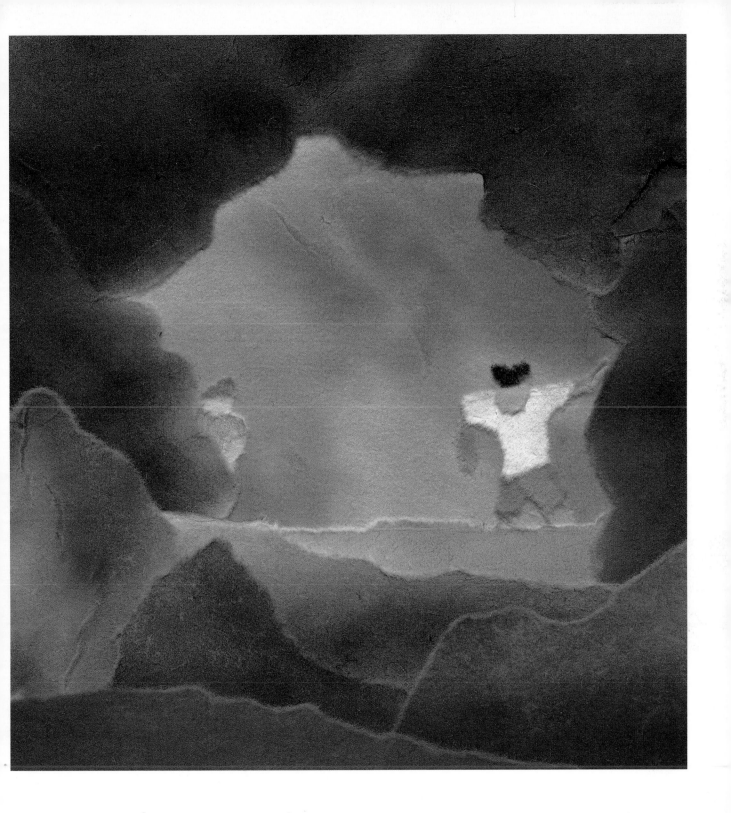

in a cave,

Or beneath a tall building—

New blues unfurl every hour.

By afternoon's end,
You may have a new friend!

Watch how the shadow
grows from your toes!

See how it hides when you go inside?

Twilight brings blue jays home for the day,

As blue as the bluefish in from the bay.

It's evening now and the sky, reborn,
Sparkles while you sleep—

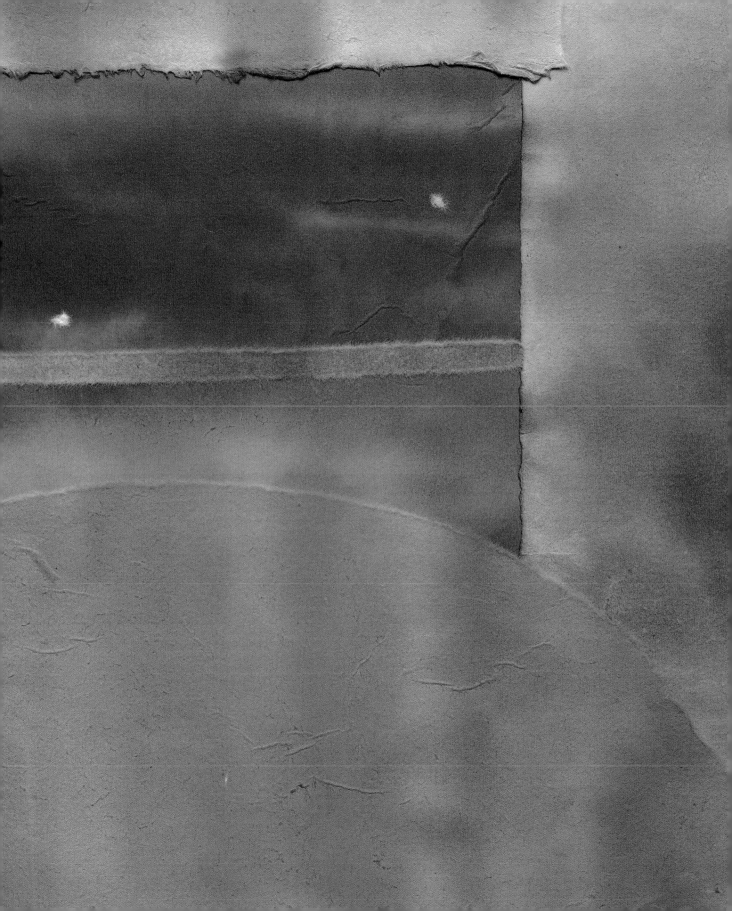

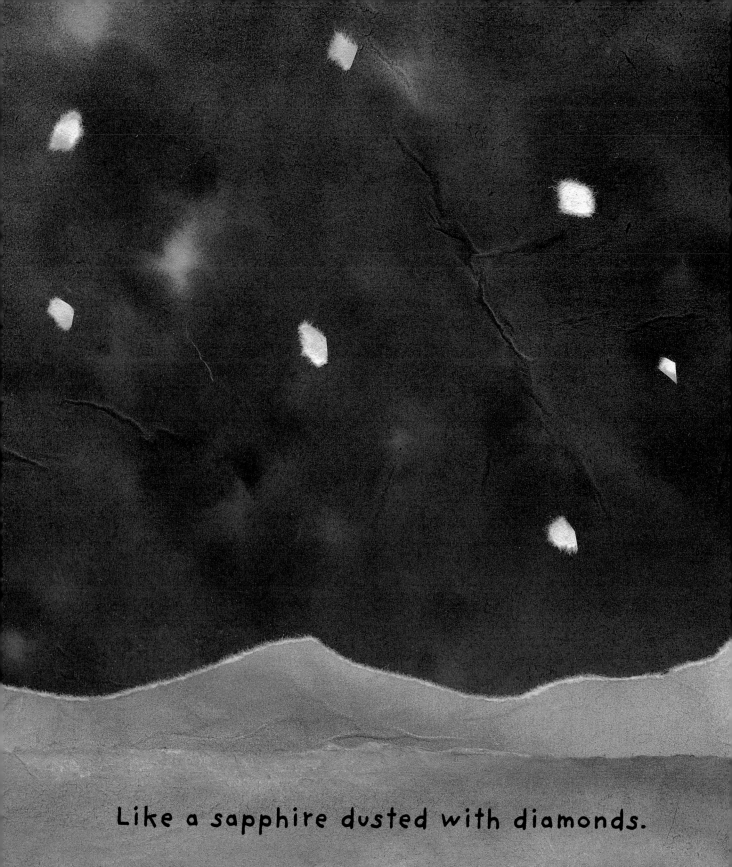

Like a sapphire dusted with diamonds.

Blue!
It surrounds you.

Blue can surprise you.

C'mon,
bring on the blue!

For Kalyn

Editors: Leslie Bockol and Meredith Wolf
Designer: Jordana Abrams
Production Manager: Lou Bilka

First edition
2 4 6 8 10 9 7 5 3 1

Library of Congress Cataloging-in-Publication Data
Whitman, Candace, date.
Bring on the blue / by Candace Whitman. — 1st ed.
p.   cm. — (My first colors)
Summary: Points out how the color blue can be found all around us, in the sky, the sea, flowers, and animals.
ISBN 0-7892-0310-3
1. Color—Juvenile literature.   2. Blue—Juvenile literature.
[1. Blue.   2. Color.]   I. Title.   II. Series: Whitman, Candace, date.
My first colors.
QC495.5.W514   1998
535.6—dc21   97-37821